DINESH D'SOUZA

WHAT'S SO GREAT ABOUT CHRISTIANITY

STUDY GUIDE

Your Guide to
Answering the New Atheists

TYNDALE HOUSE PUBLISHERS, INC.,
CAROL STREAM, ILLINOIS

Visit Tyndale's exciting Web site at www.tyndale.com.

TYNDALE and Tyndale's quill logo are registered trademarks of Tyndale House Publishers, Inc.

What's So Great about Christianity Study Guide

Copyright © 2009 by Dinesh D'Souza. All rights reserved.

Author photo copyright © by Sam Sharma. All rights reserved.

Designed by Timothy R. Botts

Scripture taken from the *Holy Bible, New International Version*®. Copyright © 1973, 1978, 1984 by International Bible Society. Used by permission of Zondervan. All rights reserved.

No part of this publication may be reproduced or transmitted in any form or by any means electronic or mechanical, including photocopy, recording, or any information storage and retrieval system now known or to be invented, without permission in writing from the publisher.

ISBN 978-1-4143-3210-9

Printed in the United States of America

15   14   13   12   11   10   09
7   6   5   4   3   2   1

CONTENTS

QUESTIONS FOR A NOTE ON THE INTERPRETATION OF SCRIPTURE

1. Why does it seem necessary in a book of this sort to include a note on how Scripture should be read?

    _____

    _____

    _____

2. What is your opinion about always reading the Bible in a literal way? Can you think of one or two Bible passages that should not be read literally?

    _____

    _____

    _____

3. The Bible uses multiple literary techniques. Why do you think Scripture is written in this way? What are the benefits of metaphor, allegory, parable, and so on? Are there any challenges in taking a literary approach?

_____

_____

_____

4. Why is it dangerous to read the Bible through the lens of contemporary assumptions? Can you think of an example of how such a reading might distort the meaning of Scripture?

_____

_____

_____

5. Do you agree with the idea of reading Scripture in a "contextual" way? Why or why not? Explain briefly your approach to reading the Bible.

_____

_____

_____

A CHALLENGE TO BELIEVERS— AND UNBELIEVERS

1. Consider 1 Peter 3:15: "Always be prepared to give an answer to everyone who asks you to give the reason for the hope that you have." Why should Christians always be prepared to do this? Give some examples of questions that might come up for which a Christian should have a ready answer.

_____

_____

_____

2. What advice would you give a Christian friend who wanted to be better prepared to talk to unbelievers about his or her faith?

_____

_____

_____

3. Can you think of a time when you felt well prepared to tell someone about your faith—or a time when you wish you had been better prepared? Describe your experience.

_____

_____

_____

4. Do you think that the biblical command to "be prepared to give an answer" is especially relevant to our time? If so, why do you think this advice might be even more important today than in the past? If not, why not?

_____

_____

_____

5. What does it mean to be "*in* the world" but not "*of* the world"? Do you think this phrase accurately describes the way you live your life? Why or why not?

_____

_____

_____

6. This preface describes the rise of a new atheism that belligerently assaults traditional Christianity. Why do you think this movement has arisen now? Have you personally encountered this new atheism? Have you ever been attacked for your faith? Describe your experience.

_____

_____

_____

7. "This is not a time for Christians to turn the other cheek." Do you agree or disagree? Explain your answer. In what circumstances should Christians turn the other cheek? What should Christians do to answer the atheists? How willing are you to do this?

   _____

   _____

   _____

8. Do you agree or disagree that Christians should focus their defense on "traditional Christianity" rather than on fundamentalism? What would be the benefits or shortcomings of such an approach?

   _____

   _____

   _____

9. "Nowhere in this book do I take Christianity for granted. My modus operandi is one of skepticism." What do you think about this approach? What are its benefits and its limitations?

   _____

   _____

   _____

10. What is the message of this chapter for atheists and unbelievers?

    _____

    _____

    _____

11. As you read *What's So Great about Christianity*, what are you hoping to discover?

_____

_____

_____

PART I

THE FUTURE OF CHRISTIANITY

THE TWILIGHT OF ATHEISM: THE GLOBAL TRIUMPH OF CHRISTIANITY

1. This chapter is about the growth of religion, and especially Christianity, around the world. Have you noticed any signs or examples of a global religious revival? If so, where do you see this happening today?

   _____

   _____

   _____

2. Would you describe yourself as *religious*? What does that term mean to you?

   _____

   _____

   _____

3. What is meant by "practical atheism"? Can someone who claims to be a Christian also be a "practical atheist"? If you're a Christian, have there been instances in your life where you've behaved as a practical atheist in spite of your belief? Is it possible to be a "practical Christian" in the same way one would be a practical atheist? What would that look like? Explain your response.

_____

_____

_____

4. What is "fundamentalism"? Why is this term inappropriate in describing Islam? Describe the difference between being a fundamentalist and being a radical.

_____

_____

_____

5. "By 'traditional' I mean religion as it has been understood and practiced over the centuries." Is this your understanding of traditional religion? How does traditional religion differ from liberal religion?

_____

_____

_____

6. "Liberal Christians are distinguished by how much intellectual and moral ground they concede to the adversaries of Christianity." Can you think of some recent examples of how liberal Christians have conceded to the secular world? Why do you suppose liberal Christianity rose in popularity for a time, and why is it now in decline?

   _____

   _____

   _____

7. Do you think that, in general, the world is becoming more religious or more secular? Why?

   _____

   _____

   _____

8. How has Christianity become a "universal religion" today? What is the new face of Christianity, and how will this affect the church as a whole?

   _____

   _____

   _____

9. Why has Christianity spread fastest in Third World countries since the end of European colonialism?

   _____

   _____

   _____

10. Do you agree that Third World Christianity is closer to the world described in the Bible? Give a few examples. As a Western believer, discuss how easy or difficult it is for you to identify personally with the problems and situations depicted in Scripture.

_____

_____

_____

11. What does Peter Berger mean by the "myth of secularization"? Do you think that this myth opens up a door of opportunity for Christians? Explain.

_____

_____

_____

12. What does it mean to be both "countercultural" and "modern"? How does this particular vantage point influence the perspective taken in *What's So Great about Christianity*? Would you describe yourself as countercultural, modern, both, or neither? Discuss your response.

_____

_____

_____

SURVIVAL OF THE SACRED: WHY RELIGION IS WINNING

1. Discuss why religion is a puzzle from an evolutionary point of view. How does religion present an intellectual stumbling block for proponents of evolutionism?

   _____

   _____

   _____

2. How does biologist E. O. Wilson hope to finally discredit traditional religion? Do you think he will succeed? Why or why not?

   _____

   _____

   _____

3. Why does it not make evolutionary sense for Christianity to have developed as a form of "wishful thinking"? Discuss Steven Pinker's quote: "A freezing person finds no comfort in believing he is warm. A person face to face with a lion is not put at ease by the conviction that he is a rabbit."[1]

_____

_____

_____

4. Do you agree with the "natural and evolutionary explanation" for the universality and persistence of religious belief described in this chapter? Why or why not?

_____

_____

_____

5. Discuss Randy Alcorn's two creation stories and the two groups of people—the secular tribe and the religious tribe—that subscribe to these stories. Which of the two tribes is more likely to survive, prosper, and multiply? Explain your answer.

_____

_____

_____

6. What evidence is there to show that secular nations are not reproducing themselves? Discuss how the trend toward smaller families in secular nations undermines a Darwinist worldview.

_____

_____

_____

7. What is the economic explanation that scholars have given in the past to explain large families? Why is this explanation inadequate? What are some alternative explanations?

_____

_____

_____

8. Discuss how the influx of immigrants from the Third World to Western countries might affect the religious direction of those countries—particularly yours. What changes might you look for in the way Christianity is practiced?

_____

_____

_____

9. In his book *Darwin's Cathedral*, David Sloan Wilson makes the point that religion offers people hope and the incentive to be moral and charitable, resulting in a more adaptive and cohesive community. How does this observation relate to the theme of this chapter—that religion is winning out over secularism?

_____

_____

_____

10. What is meant by the statement, "It is not religion but atheism that requires a Darwinian explanation"?

_____

_____

_____

GOD IS NOT GREAT: THE ATHEIST ASSAULT ON RELIGION

1. Explain your understanding of the term "atheist backlash."
   Have you seen evidence of this backlash in your community
   or country? Explain.

   _____

   _____

   _____

2. What differences, if any, do you see between agnostics and
   atheists? Do these differences matter? Why or why not?

   _____

   _____

   _____

3. What is a "bright," according to Richard Dawkins? Why are brights and other unbelievers unimpressed by the growth of religion worldwide? What does the term *bright* imply about those who disagree with the brights' perspective?

_____

_____

_____

4. Do you personally know any brights or other atheists or agnostics? If so, have you ever had a conversation with them about the existence of God? How did it go?

_____

_____

_____

5. Do you agree that atheism today marches behind the banner of science? Explain. Does this make atheism more threatening or less threatening to Christians? Why?

_____

_____

_____

6. Why does it seem that a majority of scientists are atheists? How do scientists who are Christian reconcile science and faith?

_____

_____

_____

7. Discuss what Richard Dawkins means by the statement, "Darwin made it possible to be an intellectually fulfilled atheist." Do you think it's possible to be an intellectually fulfilled Christian? Discuss your response.

_____

_____

_____

8. What is "the God of the Gaps"? Explain why this approach is often a weak argument to make in defense of God. As a believer, how would you refute this argument?

_____

_____

_____

9. What is the "ghost in the machine"? What term might Christians use instead of *ghost*? How has modern science made it difficult for many people to believe in such a "ghost"?

_____

_____

_____

10. Discuss the Enlightenment doctrines of materialism (that matter is the only reality) and naturalism (that there are no supernatural influences in nature), which form the intellectual foundation of modern atheism. What evidence of these doctrines do you see in the world today? What do these doctrines say about God?

_____

_____

_____

11. Discuss Nietzsche's "moral" critique of religion. For what purpose does he think religion was "invented"? What does he mean by "slave morality"? Do you think any of Nietzsche's ideas are still active in society today? Explain.

_____

_____

_____

12. Atheists today like to focus on the historical and contemporary crimes of religion. Are you embarrassed by the violent actions that have been taken in the name of God? Make a list of such crimes and discuss whether Christianity should take responsibility for them. What response would you give to someone who denounced Christianity based on, say, the Crusades or the Inquisition?

_____

_____

_____

13. "The War on Terror is commonly portrayed as a clash of competing extremisms, with Islamic fanaticism on one side and Christian fanaticism on the other." Do you believe this is an accurate portrayal? Why or why not? Discuss how events such as the September 11 attacks, which columnist Wendy Kaminer described as a "faith-based initiative,"[2] bolster the atheists' determination to eliminate religion altogether.

_____

_____

_____

14. What are some common themes of modern atheism? Have you seen these themes in today's world? In what way has a character such as Milton's Satan now become a so-called atheist hero? What are the goals and aspirations of the vocal contingent known as the new atheists?

   _____

   _____

   _____

15. What answer would you give to someone who says that believing in Christianity requires checking your brain at the door?

   _____

   _____

   _____

MISEDUCATING THE YOUNG: SAVING CHILDREN FROM THEIR PARENTS

1. Think about this chapter's opening quotation, in which Richard Dawkins charges that for parents to inculcate religious belief in children is a form of child abuse. Do you find this claim shocking? Explain. What do you think is his reasoning?

   _____

   _____

   _____

2. Describe how your parents influenced—or did not influence—the beliefs you hold today.

   _____

   _____

   _____

3. How would you respond if someone in authority told you that you could no longer teach religion to your children?

_____

_____

_____

4. Can the movement to promote Darwinism be viewed simply as the advocacy of science? Why or why not? What is another purpose of promoting Darwinism?

_____

_____

_____

5. How would you respond to someone who regarded religious faith as a form of mental illness?

_____

_____

_____

6. Discuss the "larger educational project" that Darwinism seems to be spearheading. What are its implications for you and your children?

_____

_____

_____

7. How does atheist Daniel Dennett want to preserve religions? What, from an atheist point of view, would be the purpose of this?

   _____

   _____

   _____

8. "The cosmos is all there is or ever was or ever will be."[3] Do you think Carl Sagan's maxim is a scientific statement? Explain your response.

   _____

   _____

   _____

9. What is apatheism? In what way do atheists consider it an "achievement"? Do you know any people who would fit this category? What are the signs that someone is an apatheist?

   _____

   _____

   _____

10. How do atheists expect science to replace religion as an object of human veneration? Note any instances where you've already seen this happening.

   _____

   _____

   _____

11. How does philosopher Richard Rorty hope to discredit what he calls "fundamentalist" religion among students? Is this approach likely to work? Has it begun working already? Share any examples you have of teachers or professors who have tried to discredit religious views.

_____

_____

_____

12. Discuss how adolescent sexuality can be a vehicle for atheists to promote their agenda. Does this idea seem plausible to you? Explain.

_____

_____

_____

13. If Christian parents are financing the destruction of their own beliefs and values, as the chapter suggests, what steps can they take to turn the tide?

_____

_____

_____

14. Discuss how you, as a parent, might be prepared to give an answer in the following situations:

• Your first-grader comes home from school, wide-eyed with wonder, relating a tale of how human beings are descended from monkeys.

_____

_____

_____

- Your teen comes home from high school upset that he was berated by a teacher for wearing his favorite T-shirt that has a Christian message printed on it.

_____

_____

_____

- Your daughter, home from college on break, refuses to go to church and refers to Christianity as a childish myth that she has outgrown.

_____

_____

_____

15. Think back to your own school years. Do you think the push toward atheism in the schools was as strong then as it is now? Why or why not?

_____

_____

_____

16. If you are rearing children today, what do you think of the education your child is receiving? Were you aware of the push toward atheism in schools and colleges and the trend toward diminishing the parent's role in teaching children about religion? Are you satisfied with the approach you've taken so far regarding your child's schooling? As a result of reading this chapter, are you planning to make any changes to the way your child is being educated?

_____

_____

_____

PART II

CHRISTIANITY AND THE WEST

RENDER UNTO CAESAR: THE SPIRITUAL BASIS OF LIMITED GOVERNMENT

1. The chapter opens with a quote from leading atheist philosopher Jürgen Habermas. Why do you think this quote was chosen? Are you surprised to learn that Habermas is an atheist?

   _____

   _____

   _____

2. What is the "problem of the Muslim *madrassas*," and how does America's problem compare/contrast with it? Do you know of any public schools in which the Bible is studied?

   _____

   _____

   _____

3. How are Westerners today "aliens in their own civilization"? Do you think this is a religious shortcoming or a shortcoming of a different kind? Explain your response.

_____

_____

_____

4. What bias do terms such as *Dark Ages, Renaissance,* and *Enlightenment* suggest? Discuss whether your impressions of these terms were confirmed or challenged by this chapter.

_____

_____

_____

5. Why might the framers of the European Union's constitution be reluctant to list Christianity as a founding influence on their new form of union? What has Europe lost (or what does it stand to lose) by eliminating Christianity from its foundation?

_____

_____

_____

6. Do you think the United States is heading in the same direction as Europe in terms of Christianity? What would be the implications of such a trend? What can be done to stop or reverse a move toward secularization?

_____

_____

_____

7. How has Christianity shaped the values and institutions that secular people cherish? Give some examples. Why is it important for more people to know about the Christian beginnings of many of our cultural values? What will happen to these values if Christianity is marginalized?

_____

_____

_____

8. What is Edward Gibbon's argument against Christianity? How is it refuted here? In your own words, think of a response you could give to someone who holds Christianity responsible for the fall of classical civilization.

_____

_____

_____

9. The chapter includes some examples of great art, architecture, literature, and music that have been inspired by Christianity. Can you add your own examples to this list? Do you think that such works would have been created even if Christianity had never existed? Explain your answer.

_____

_____

_____

10. Discuss how "Christianity introduced not only a new religion but a new conception of religion."

_____

_____

_____

11. When atheists describe religion as a human invention, in what sense are they accurately portraying the deities of pagan polytheism? How is the God of Judaism and Christianity different?

_____

_____

_____

12. List two important differences between Jewish and Christian monotheism. Have you observed any differences between the religious practices of Jews and Christians? If so, what are they? Why did the Romans tolerate Jewish monotheism but prohibit Christianity?

_____

_____

_____

13. How is monotheism practiced differently in Islamic countries?

_____

_____

_____

14. What answer would you give to someone who said, "All the major religions believe in the same God"?

_____

_____

_____

15. Talk about the connection between Augustine's two cities (the earthly city and the heavenly city) and the modern concept of limited government. Do you agree that the separation of church and state is, at its root, a Christian concept? If so, is this idea surprising to you? Explain your response.

    _____

    _____

    _____

16. "Somehow freedom for religious expression has become freedom from religious expression." Do you agree? Discuss any examples of religious intolerance you have seen or experienced that was directed at Christians.

    _____

    _____

    _____

17. How did the concept of the separation of church and state persist through the centuries of Christian history? Do you agree that even violations of this separation often arose from commendable motives? Why or why not?

    _____

    _____

    _____

18. Distinguish between "tolerance" and "freedom of conscience."
    How was the European idea of tolerance transformed into the
    American idea of religious freedom? Do you think the tradi-
    tional definition of *tolerance* is the same one used in society
    today? Explain.

    _____

    _____

    _____

19. Why do you suppose the American founders sought to exclude
    theology from the province of government and law while making
    morality central to both? Do you think that the government
    and judicial systems the founders intended are the same as or
    different from the ones we have today? Why?

    _____

    _____

    _____

20. In what way has the concept of separation of church and state
    been abused? Give one or two specific examples.

    _____

    _____

    _____

THE EVIL THAT I WOULD NOT: CHRISTIANITY AND HUMAN FALLIBILITY

1. Contrast Plato's diagnosis of the problem of evil with Paul's (Romans 7:19). In your opinion, who is right? Why?

   _____

   _____

   _____

2. How did Christianity transform the way in which the "low" or ordinary man is viewed? Discuss how this was a radically countercultural view for its time. What Christian views might be considered countercultural today?

   _____

   _____

   _____

3. In what ways did Plato and Aristotle diminish the importance
   of the family? Do you think the family is still being diminished
   today? Give some examples.

   _____

   _____

   _____

4. How did Christianity (both Catholic and Protestant) affirm the
   family's importance? What can be done today to preserve the
   importance of the family?

   _____

   _____

   _____

5. Name two ways in which Christianity shaped our modern
   concept of the rule of law. Why does this matter? Discuss
   how it is possible, if Christianity formed the basis of our laws,
   that Christianity is now being squeezed out of the courts and
   public life.

   _____

   _____

   _____

6. Review Mark 10:43 and Luke 22:27 on servant leadership.
   What are some of the characteristics of a servant leader? Share
   examples of servant leadership in action that you have seen in
   ministry, community, business, politics, or family life. Do you
   consider yourself to be a servant leader? Explain.

   _____

   _____

   _____

7. "Capitalism civilizes greed in much the same way that marriage civilizes lust." Do you agree with this statement? Why or why not? Have you ever thought of capitalism in those terms before?

_____

_____

_____

8. Discuss how the idea of progress is a Christian legacy. Is that how progress is viewed today? Explain your response.

_____

_____

_____

9. What response would you give to someone who said, "Christians are no more compassionate than anyone else"? What has been your experience among people you know? Support your answer with examples.

_____

_____

_____

CREATED EQUAL: THE ORIGIN OF HUMAN DIGNITY

1. What do you believe about the equality of all human beings? Does being equal mean being the same? Explain.

   _____

   _____

   _____

2. Why did Nietzsche call the concept of equality "crazy"? What effect has this "crazy" concept had on the course of Western society?

   _____

   _____

   _____

3. In what sense did Jefferson mean it was "self-evident" that all men are created equal? What kind of equality was he writing about? If it is self-evident, why do so many cultures around the world not believe that all human beings are equal?

_____

_____

_____

4. How can the preciousness and equal worth of every human life be considered a Christian idea? How did Martin Luther interpret this idea? Share some examples of how the value of human life is still being debated today.

_____

_____

_____

5. Give some examples of how ancient Greece and Rome depreciated human life and exploited women. Have you seen or experienced similar attitudes today? Explain.

_____

_____

_____

6. How did Christianity modify patriarchy and elevate the status of women? Why do some secularists accuse Christianity of oppressing women?

_____

_____

_____

7. Written when slavery was a universal institution, the Bible seems to have tolerated the practice. When the Bible instructs slaves to obey their masters, is there an implied approval of slavery? What answer would you give to someone who says the Bible endorses slavery?

    _____

    _____

    _____

8. Who were the first Christians in the modern era to oppose slavery in principle? On what basis did they do this? Why do you suppose many secularists don't give credit to Christianity for the abolishment of slavery?

    _____

    _____

    _____

9. Had you realized that the American Revolution and the Civil War were both preceded by sweeping religious awakenings? What role did the two Great Awakenings play in these key events of American history?

    _____

    _____

    _____

10. Was the civil rights movement of the twentieth century inspired by Christianity or by secular values? Discuss.

    _____

    _____

    _____

11. Discuss how secular concepts of human rights, such as those of John Rawls and Jeremy Bentham, were themselves derived from Christian assumptions. How do you think a secular human-rights advocate would respond to this?

_____

_____

_____

12. What are the core principles of the "just war" theory? Discuss how these principles are related to the core teachings of Christianity.

_____

_____

_____

13. What was the ancient view of freedom, according to Benjamin Constant? How does it differ from our modern ideas of freedom? Why does this matter to us?

_____

_____

_____

14. What was Nietzsche's warning to Western societies? Do you think Western culture can get rid of Christianity and yet keep its values? Why or why not? What secular trends seem to support your answer?

_____

_____

_____

PART III

CHRISTIANITY AND SCIENCE

CHRISTIANITY AND REASON: THE THEOLOGICAL ROOTS OF SCIENCE

1. What role does reason play in your beliefs about God? Explain.

   _____

   _____

   _____

2. Why is it significant that "science as an organized, sustained enterprise" arose originally in Western civilization?

   _____

   _____

   _____

3. Given that many of the earliest scientists were Christians, how do you think society has reached a point where science and religion seem to be at odds with each other?

_____

_____

_____

4. Define *animism* and describe how it gave rise to polytheistic religion. Do you think there are still traces of animism around today? If so, give some examples.

_____

_____

_____

5. How is reason central to Christianity in a way that it is not central to Judaism and Islam? What do you think this means for Christian believers?

_____

_____

_____

6. Augustine theorized that God created time along with the universe. Why is this an important concept for Christians to understand? What does this tell us about time and eternity?

_____

_____

_____

7. "If God created the universe, what created God?"[4] Atheists often use arguments like this to rebut Aquinas's ideas about causation. What would Aquinas say in reply to them? How would you respond to someone who believes in cause and effect but not in God?

   _____

   _____

   _____

8. Can you restate Anselm's argument for the existence of God? Do you find it convincing? Why or why not? Why does Anselm's argument apply only to God and not to unicorns and flying spaghetti monsters?

   _____

   _____

   _____

9. What bearing do the ancient theological arguments of Augustine, Aquinas, and Anselm have on the way we practice and talk about our faith today?

   _____

   _____

   _____

10. After reading this chapter, do you feel better prepared to give an answer to an atheist who challenges your faith? Explain.

    _____

    _____

    _____

FROM LOGOS TO COSMOS: CHRISTIANITY AND THE INVENTION OF INVENTION

1. How do you define *faith*? How does faith shape what you believe about God and the universe?

   _____

   _____

   _____

2. "The greatest idea of modern science is based not on reason but on faith." Discuss what this "greatest idea" is and how it is based on faith.

   _____

   _____

   _____

3. Why is *faith* looked down upon in the scientific community? Do you consider faith a vice or a virtue? Why?

_____

_____

_____

4. If God did not create nature, can you think of a reason why nature should be rational and lawful? Explain.

_____

_____

_____

5. How did Christianity contribute to the idea of a "disenchanted" universe? What difference could this concept make when discussing faith matters with an atheist?

_____

_____

_____

6. How does the Muslim thinker Abu Hamed al-Ghazali's idea of a miraculous universe differ from the Christian idea? What is the difference between al-Ghazali's idea of miracles and yours?

_____

_____

_____

7. If the earliest and greatest universities in the West started as Christian institutions, what happened to them? Have you seen or heard any evidence that these institutions are no longer Christian? Discuss.

    _____

    _____

    _____

8. Explain how the Reformation contributed to the development of modern science. How did the first professional scientists view their work? Do you think scientists today view their work in a similar way?

    _____

    _____

    _____

9. Name some leading scientists who were also Christian. How did they view their vocation? Can you describe what some of them accomplished in their fields?

    _____

    _____

    _____

10. Do you know of any scientists who are atheists? Describe their accomplishments.

    _____

    _____

    _____

11. Describe how Kepler's Christianity helped him to discover what he saw as a divine scheme of planetary rotation far more subtle and beautiful than anyone had previously imagined.

_____

_____

_____

12. "In every true searcher of nature there is a kind of religious reverence."[5] What does this statement by Einstein mean? Does it imply a belief in God?

_____

_____

_____

13. What points in this chapter could you use when talking with someone who holds that science and theology have no common ground?

_____

_____

_____

AN ATHEIST FABLE:
REOPENING THE GALILEO CASE

1. Read the first paragraph of the chapter, which mentions several claims by atheist writers about Christianity and the persecution of scientists. These claims include no fewer than five errors of fact. Can you cite some of them? Do you remember hearing any of these fallacies when you were in school? Why do you think they are so seldom refuted?

   _____

   _____

   _____

2. Who are the two American writers who invented the so-called war between science and religion? Why have their theories endured, even though the writers themselves have been discredited?

   _____

   _____

   _____

3. Name two ways in which ancient and medieval people were able to determine, without a telescope or other instruments, that the earth is round. How does this discredit the idea that the medieval church insisted the earth was flat?

_____

_____

_____

4. Why does the execution of Giordano Bruno, often cited as an example of church persecution of scientific thought, show nothing of the sort?

_____

_____

_____

5. For centuries, Christians generally held that the earth was stationary and that the sun revolved around the earth. Why do you think they held this view? Was this a uniquely Christian belief?

_____

_____

_____

6. What does the Bible say about heliocentrism?

_____

_____

_____

7. If Scripture does not take a clear position on planetary motion, what does that teach us about how to evaluate scientific theories when they seem to contradict our general conception of creation?

_____

_____

_____

8. Many history textbooks include accounts of events that never actually took place. See, for instance, the examples cited in the chapter: Thomas Henry Huxley's fictional exchange with bishop Samuel Wilberforce; Galileo's alleged experiments in Pisa, and his apocryphal response to his inquisitors. If these incidents were fabricated or exaggerated, how do such falsehoods make their way into textbooks and be taught as true? How can we make sure that truth is being taught?

_____

_____

_____

9. Consider Cardinal Bellarmine's instruction to Galileo not to teach or promote heliocentrism. Do you agree with Bellarmine's reasons for giving this instruction? Why or why not?

_____

_____

_____

10. What caused Galileo to go back on his word and write a book publicly defending the heliocentric theory? Do you think he was justified in doing so? Explain.

_____

_____

_____

11. Give three historical reasons why the Catholic Church reacted so strongly to Galileo. Can you think of another example of a scientific theory that raised such controversy?

_____

_____

_____

12. Galileo was never convicted of heresy. What was his actual offense? Was he guilty?

_____

_____

_____

13. Atheist images of Galileo cowering in a dungeon and being tortured by the church are pure fabrications. What ideological purpose do such fabrications serve?

_____

_____

_____

14. When did heliocentrism come to be accepted as scientific fact? How then should we judge Galileo and his critics?

    _____

    _____

    _____

15. What can Christians learn from the Galileo case? Is there anything about this case that the church should have done differently? If so, what?

    _____

    _____

    _____

16. Based on this chapter, what answers are you prepared to give to someone who believes one or more of the myths surrounding the supposed conflict between science and the church?

    _____

    _____

    _____

PART IV

THE ARGUMENT FROM DESIGN

A UNIVERSE WITH A BEGINNING: GOD AND THE ASTRONOMERS

1. Do you believe that the design of nature points to a Creator? Discuss.

   _____

   _____

   _____

2. Do you agree that the idea of an eternal universe (one that has always been) supports atheism? What is the significance of the scientific discovery that the universe indeed had a beginning?

   _____

   _____

   _____

3. Where did scientists get the idea that the universe is expanding? What does an expanding universe indicate about the origin of the universe?

   _____

   _____

   _____

4. Briefly explain the Big Bang theory as you understand it. Does the notion of a universe nearly fifteen billion years old trouble you? Why or why not?

_____

_____

_____

5. "Before the Big Bang, there were no laws of physics." Why can't the laws of physics predate the formation of the universe? How could this idea support the argument for a Creator?

_____

_____

_____

6. Why did the ancient Greeks hold that the universe has always existed? Evaluate their maxim _ex nihilo, nihil_: "out of nothing, there is nothing."

_____

_____

_____

7. What does the Bible say about how the universe came to be? How does the biblical account compare to the Big Bang theory?

_____

_____

_____

8. "I have no need of that hypothesis." Who said this, and why? Do you think he was correct?

_____

_____

_____

9. Atheists often compare the Christian "creation myth" to those of other ancient religions. How does the biblical account of creation differ from those of other religions?

_____

_____

_____

10. Christians have disagreed over the centuries about whether the universe was created in six literal calendar days. What do you believe, and why? Does it matter to your faith whether God created the universe in six twenty-four-hour periods? Why or why not?

_____

_____

_____

11. How does the modern Big Bang theory resolve one of the apparent contradictions in the book of Genesis? What is this seeming contradiction, and do you agree that it needs to be resolved? Explain.

_____

_____

_____

12. "I am not citing the Bible to prove that God created the universe. I am citing it to show that the biblical account of how the universe was created is substantially correct." What are the merits or deficiencies of approaching the creation discussion in this way? How does this method inform our approach to apologetics? How might you use this same approach?

_____

_____

_____

13. "Everything that begins to exist has a cause. The universe began to exist. Therefore the universe has a cause. That cause we call God." If you were an atheist, how might you dispute this reasoning? Does it help you formulate a valid argument for the existence of a Creator?

_____

_____

_____

14. How can we know that the universe had a supernatural, rather than a natural, cause? How would you respond to someone who endorses only a natural cause?

_____

_____

_____

15. How can our conclusions about God's existence as Creator help us to infer some of his divine attributes?

_____

_____

_____

A DESIGNER PLANET:
MAN'S SPECIAL PLACE IN CREATION

1. In what ways did the Copernican revolution spill over from science into philosophy?

   _____

   _____

   _____

2. In your opinion, why does it matter that we understand humanity's place in creation?

   _____

   _____

   _____

3. What is the principle of mediocrity? How did it originate? Is this a scientific principle? What Christian idea is challenged by the principle of mediocrity?

_____

_____

_____

4. Define the anthropic principle. How does it reverse the Copernican revolution and undermine the principle of mediocrity? What does this mean for humanity?

_____

_____

_____

5. Why do you think it took scientists so long to stumble upon the notion of a fine-tuned universe? What simple questions and answers brought physicists to their conclusion?

_____

_____

_____

6. Name some of the numerical constants that underlie the physical properties of the universe. Give an example of how the slightest change in one of these values would make it impossible to have a universe like ours that can sustain living beings like us.

_____

_____

_____

7. How does the fine-tuned universe suggest not only a Creator, but a Creator who cares personally for us? Can you find any Scripture verses to support this idea?

_____

_____

_____

8. Briefly discuss the three responses to the anthropic principle given in the chapter: Lucky Us, Multiple Universes, and the Designer Universe. Do you know anyone who believes any of these explanations? If so, describe how he or she might talk about God and religion.

_____

_____

_____

9. Some atheists have suggested that our presence as humans on earth is simply a fortunate accident. Why is this an invalid argument, and how does it misrepresent the anthropic principle?

_____

_____

_____

10. Some atheists argue that our existence on earth is simply the product of a "selection effect." In the words of Richard Dawkins, "If the planet were suitable for another kind of life, it is that kind of life that would have evolved here."[6] What's wrong with this reasoning?

_____

_____

_____

11. Discuss how the possibility of multiple universes gives scientific plausibility to the Christian concepts of heaven and hell.

_____

_____

_____

12. What is the principle of Occam's razor? How does it speak against the theory of multiple universes?

_____

_____

_____

13. "It seems that to abolish one unobservable God, it takes an infinite number of unobservable substitutes."[7] Do you think physicist Stephen Barr is right about why many scientists seem so eager to embrace the theory of multiple universes? Why or why not?

_____

_____

_____

14. "If the divine underpinning of the laws [of nature] is removed," writes physicist Paul Davies, "their existence becomes a profound mystery. Where do they come from?"[8] Brainstorm possible answers to this question and discuss.

_____

_____

_____

15. Having read this chapter, what response can you give to someone who questions humanity's importance in the universe?

_____

_____

_____

16. Do you think believers and unbelievers can find common ground to discuss the origin of the universe and our place in it? Explain your answer.

_____

_____

_____

PALEY WAS RIGHT: EVOLUTION AND THE ARGUMENT FROM DESIGN

1. How comfortable are you with discussing evolution and creation? Do you tend to avoid the topic or embrace it? Explain your response.

   _____

   _____

   _____

2. Briefly summarize William Paley's famous argument about the divine "watchmaker." Name two premises on which this argument depends for its validity. Do you think Paley's argument holds water? Why or why not?

   _____

   _____

   _____

3. What does Richard Dawkins mean in calling evolution "the blind watchmaker"? What does it tell you about Dawkins's opinion of man's origins?

_____

_____

_____

4. What is social Darwinism? Identify some of its consequences in contemporary Western society.

_____

_____

_____

5. Do you believe that Darwinism is incompatible with belief in Christ? Explain your answer.

_____

_____

_____

6. What evidence have you seen that there is an antireligious thrust in Darwinism? Give some examples.

_____

_____

_____

7. Does evolution contradict the claims of the Bible? Do you agree with the position taken in this chapter? Why or why not?

_____

_____

_____

8. Discuss the possibility that our bodily frame may be the product of evolution, but our soul is breathed into us by God.

_____

_____

_____

9. Have you heard people say that the main opposition to evolution from the beginning came from Christians? Discuss why this is a distortion of history and identify people who have objected to evolution on purely scientific grounds.

_____

_____

_____

10. Who are some prominent Christians, past and present, who have seen no conflict between evolution and Christianity? Why has this issue proved to be so divisive among Christians? Has it been an issue for you? Why or why not?

_____

_____

_____

11. In your view, what are the two strongest arguments for evolution? What are two of the strongest objections that can be made against the theory?

_____

_____

_____

12. Biologist Stephen Jay Gould once described Richard Dawkins and Daniel Dennett as "Darwinian fundamentalists." What is meant by this term?

_____

_____

_____

13. Even if the theory of evolution is true, it cannot account for "three massive features of life." What are the three big questions that evolution cannot answer?

_____

_____

_____

14. What two features of a cell defy natural explanation and are presumed to exist before any evolution can take place?

_____

_____

_____

15. Why are consciousness and rationality such a problem for evolution to explain? Can you think of any explanations that might work?

_____

_____

_____

16. What is meant by the terms "God of the Gaps" and "atheism of the gaps"? What is a reasonable alternative to these arguments? Can you think of ways in which you could use this reasoning to support your view of evolution or creation?

_____

_____

_____

17. "Evolution itself requires a finely tuned designer universe." Why is this significant? What questions does a designer universe raise for the evolutionist?

_____

_____

_____

18. Examine physicist Stephen Barr's argument that a watch-making factory is something even more remarkable, and in need of explanation, than a single watch. How does Barr's perspective demonstrate that the "argument from design" for God is stronger today than ever before?

_____

_____

_____

19. What is the distinction between scientific evolution and Darwinism? Which theory presents more of a problem for Christians? Should Christians embrace the former while rejecting the latter? Why or why not?

_____

_____

_____

20. "Instead of suing to get theories of creationism and intelligent design into the science classroom, Christians should be suing to get atheist interpretations of Darwin out." Is this a good strategy? What would it accomplish? Explain your response.

_____

_____

_____

21. As a result of reading this chapter, do you feel better equipped to talk to someone about evolution versus creationism? Explain.

_____

_____

_____

THE GENESIS PROBLEM: THE METHODOLOGICAL ATHEISM OF SCIENCE

1. How open do you think you are to new ideas? How open do you think most scientists are?

   _____

   _____

   _____

2. What is the "serious problem" with our understanding of modern science?

   _____

   _____

   _____

3. Why is the attempt to explain everything scientifically inadequate and unreasonable?

_____

_____

_____

4. Biologist Douglas Erwin says that "a fundamental presumption" of science is "no miracles allowed."[9] Explain why this would or would not be a reasonable position for scientists to take.

_____

_____

_____

5. Given that science was originally built on a Christian foundation, how did it become so secular that many of today's scientists refuse to allow for any supernatural explanations?

_____

_____

_____

6. What is biologist Francis Crick's theory of the origin of life on earth? In your opinion, is Crick's theory more or less valid than other theories, for example, that "some combination of chemicals must have proved the right one"?

_____

_____

_____

7. What is the logic behind Richard Dawkins's claim that we shouldn't worry about gaps in the fossil record? Do you agree or disagree with Dawkins? Explain.

_____

_____

_____

8. Define *naturalism* and *materialism*. Does modern science provide empirical support for these two doctrines? Explain.

_____

_____

_____

9. Discuss biologist Richard Lewontin's statement that he and his fellow scientists "are forced by our a priori commitment to material causes to create an apparatus of investigation and a set of concepts that produce material explanations, no matter how counter-intuitive, no matter how mystifying to the uninitiated."[10] Why this commitment to absolute materialism as an article of faith?

_____

_____

_____

10. Contrast methodological atheism and philosophical atheism. How do they both differ from theism?

_____

_____

_____

11. Is methodological atheism acceptable as a working principle of modern science? Why or why not? What is your opinion of this?

_____

_____

_____

12. Physicist John Polkinghorne gives an example that shows the limitations of understanding phenomena in a purely scientific way, ignoring intentional or purposive explanations. Can you think of other examples to make this point?

_____

_____

_____

13. Is scientific truth erroneous, or is it incomplete? If it's incomplete, what does the scientific account of reality leave out?

_____

_____

_____

14. What have you learned in this chapter that will help you give an answer to someone who wants to use science to explain everything? Explain.

_____

_____

_____

PART V

CHRISTIANITY AND PHILOSOPHY

THE WORLD BEYOND OUR SENSES: KANT AND THE LIMITS OF REASON

1. What are the "two levels of reality" that the great religions of the world have always recognized? How is human understanding limited, and what difference, if any, does this make to faith?

   _____

   _____

   _____

2. What is the "Enlightenment fallacy" that Immanuel Kant called into question? Have you fallen into the same trap yourself? Explain.

   _____

   _____

   _____

3. Is our experience of external reality the same as reality itself? Discuss the answers to this question given by Locke, Berkeley, and Hume. Which explanation seems the most plausible to you?

_____

_____

_____

4. What does Kant mean by his famous terms *noumenon* and *phenomenon*? Give some examples to illustrate. Do you think a Christian should be familiar with Kant's philosophy and terminology? Why or why not?

_____

_____

_____

5. Is Kant arguing that human experience is an illusion? If not, what is he trying to say about the capacity of reason to comprehend reality?

_____

_____

_____

6. How difficult are Kant's ideas to grasp? Do you find them sensible or counterintuitive? What scientific precedent did Kant himself invoke to show the limitations of common sense?

_____

_____

_____

7. What is the empiricist fallacy? Why does it matter to Christian believers?

_____

_____

_____

8. Critics sometimes challenge Kant by saying that, because all humans experience the same external reality, our senses are reliable instruments for capturing reality. What is wrong with this argument?

_____

_____

_____

9. If Kant is affirming what Christianity and other world religions have maintained for centuries, then what is novel or unique about his arguments?

_____

_____

_____

IN THE BELLY OF THE WHALE: WHY MIRACLES ARE POSSIBLE

1. Why is the issue of miracles of special importance to Christians? Have you witnessed any miracles in your own life?

   _____

   _____

   _____

2. Biologist Stephen Jay Gould argues that religion does not conflict with science because religion focuses on values whereas science focuses on facts. How does atheist Richard Dawkins show the limitations of this argument?

   _____

   _____

   _____

3. How do liberal Christians deal with the issue of miracles in an age of science? What is the danger of conceding that the miracles of Jesus never actually happened?

_____

_____

_____

4. Examine philosopher David Hume's four-part argument against miracles. In seeking to vindicate miracles, which of the four links in Hume's logic seems the flimsiest to you? Explain your response.

_____

_____

_____

5. What do logical positivists believe? Do you recognize the signs of logical positivism in contemporary society?

_____

_____

_____

6. What is the importance of Immanuel Kant's assertion that "mathematical truths are not analytic"? How does this apply to our understanding of science and miracles?

_____

_____

_____

7. Why aren't scientific laws verifiable? Consider the example that water boils at 212 degrees Fahrenheit. Is this always and everywhere true? If so, how could this not be verifiable?

_____

_____

_____

8. Discuss how the example of black swans illustrates Hume's point that no amount of empirical observations, however large, can establish a general conclusion that is true as a matter of logic.

_____

_____

_____

9. What is Hume's problem with the law of cause and effect? Do you agree that even though two things are always observed to occur together, we cannot infer that the first one is the necessary cause of the second? Why or why not?

_____

_____

_____

10. Astronomer Neil deGrasse Tyson notes that "science's big-time success rests on the fact that it works."[11] Do you think he has a point? What are the limitations of this point?

_____

_____

_____

11. What does philosopher Karl Popper mean when he says that science cannot verify theories, but it can falsify them? How might this apply to faith?

_____

_____

_____

12. "Miracles can be dismissed only if scientific laws are necessarily true—if they admit of no exceptions." Given this, how can we show the possibility of miracles?

_____

_____

_____

13. "Obviously, if God exists, miracles are possible." Discuss how God can act both within and beyond nature to produce miraculous effects.

_____

_____

_____

A SKEPTIC'S WAGER: PASCAL AND THE REASONABLENESS OF FAITH

1. What do you make of the phrase "the reasonableness of faith"? Should faith be reasonable? Explain your answer.

   _____

   _____

   _____

2. Biologist Stephen Jay Gould says that nothing could be more antithetical to science than Jesus' statement to Thomas, "Because you have seen me, you have believed; blessed are those who have not seen and yet have believed."[12] What is admirable about believing without seeing?

   _____

   _____

   _____

3. In what way is religious faith in a different category from the kind of faith we exercise when we travel by plane or believe statements we cannot personally verify?

    _____

    _____

    _____

4. Kant argues that on issues that reason cannot explain, it is not unreasonable to have faith. What do you make of this argument? What examples does Kant have in mind here?

    _____

    _____

    _____

5. What is wrong with Christopher Hitchens's statement that "what can be asserted without evidence can also be dismissed without evidence"?[13]

    _____

    _____

    _____

6. What is the difference between belief and knowledge? Do you agree that there is an element of agnosticism even among believers and that "doubt is the proper habit of mind for the religious believer"? Why or why not?

    _____

    _____

    _____

7. Why should we bother to try to learn about things that reason cannot figure out? In your opinion, what important questions fall into this category?

_____

_____

_____

8. In formulating his famous wager, Pascal argued that sometimes in life we cannot get full information and yet we have to choose. Think of some situations where this is true.

_____

_____

_____

9. What are the downside risks, according to Pascal, of accepting versus rejecting God?

_____

_____

_____

10. Is Pascal right that, given the risks, every reasonable person should cast his vote for God? Why or why not?

_____

_____

_____

11. How did Pascal account for "the hiddenness of God"? Have you ever wondered why God doesn't reveal Himself in an indisputably obvious way to all mankind? Discuss your response.

_____

_____

_____

12. Pascal seems to show why we should accept God, but does his argument show which God we should accept? Does Pascal's argument point to the Christian God as opposed to the gods of other religions? Explain.

_____

_____

_____

13. Discuss your response to the prayer of the skeptic.

_____

_____

_____

PART VI

CHRISTIANITY AND SUFFERING

RETHINKING THE INQUISITION: THE EXAGGERATED CRIMES OF RELIGION

1. Discuss atheist Steven Weinberg's statement, "Good people will do good things and bad people will do bad things, but for good people to do bad things—that takes religion."[14]

_____

_____

_____

2. Do you agree that the Crusades were simply an attempt to recover the heartland of Christianity and defend it against militant Islam, or were the Crusades a violation of Christian principles? Explain.

_____

_____

_____

3. What does historian Henry Kamen mean by the phrase
   "Inventing the Inquisition"?[15] Is he suggesting the Inquisition
   never happened?

   _____

   _____

   _____

4. What are some examples, past and present, of conflicts that
   are attributed to religion that were not primarily motivated by
   religious differences? How and why do you think these conflicts
   gained the reputation of being rooted in religion?

   _____

   _____

   _____

5. Evaluate Sam Harris's attempt to ascribe religious motives to
   the inventors of suicide bombing, the Tamil Tigers. How persua-
   sive is his argument?

   _____

   _____

   _____

6. The chapter concludes by contrasting violence with the gentle
   and peaceful spirit of Christ. Do you agree that violence in the
   name of Christianity is alien to the spirit and teachings of Christ?
   Why or why not?

   _____

   _____

   _____

A LICENSE TO KILL: ATHEISM AND THE MASS MURDERS OF HISTORY

1. Richard Dawkins argues that "individual atheists may do evil things but they don't do evil things *in the name of atheism*."[16] What's wrong with this argument?

   _____

   _____

   _____

2. What did Nazism have in common with Communism? In what sense were both secular ideologies seeking to replace traditional religion and morality?

   _____

   _____

   _____

3. Do you agree with Daniel Dennett's standard that religious and philosophical systems must be held at least partly responsible for the crimes committed in their name? Should Islam, for example, bear some responsibility for al Qaeda? Why or why not?

    _____

    _____

    _____

4. Answer Sam Harris's argument that Maoism and Stalinism were really religious systems and thus the crimes of Mao and Stalin can be counted as religious crimes. Explain why you agree or disagree.

    _____

    _____

    _____

5. Atheist Web sites routinely describe Hitler as a Christian and point out that he was baptized as a Catholic, he never left the church, and he wrote in *Mein Kampf,* "By defending myself against the Jew, I am fighting for the work of the Lord."[17] How would you respond to someone who described Hitler as a Christian?

    _____

    _____

    _____

6. Give an argument to show that Hitler's anti-Semitism was not religious but secular.

    _____

    _____

    _____

7. According to historian Richard Weikart, what were the two main intellectual influences on Hitler and the Nazis? How does Weikart's argument turn the tables on atheists who suggest that Hitler was a Christian?

_____

_____

_____

8. If it's true that atheism is responsible for many of the mass murders of history, why do you think this is so? Is there something about atheism that produces such results?

_____

_____

_____

PART VII

CHRISTIANITY AND MORALITY

NATURAL LAW AND DIVINE LAW: THE OBJECTIVE FOUNDATIONS OF MORALITY

1. The apostle Paul writes in Romans 2:14, "When Gentiles, who do not have the law, do by nature things required by the law, they show that the requirements of the law are written on their hearts."[18] What is Paul speaking about here?

   _____

   _____

   _____

2. Consider Richard Dawkins's description of the God of the Old Testament as a genocidal maniac. This is a moral assault on God's goodness and mercy and justice. How would you counter this charge, which is often made by today's atheists?

   _____

   _____

   _____

3. Many atheists will say they are just as ethical, if not more so, than Christians. At the very least, they contend, there is nothing about religion that gives one a monopoly on virtue, and morality is quite possible without the presumption of God or religion. Do you agree or disagree? Discuss. Do you believe morality must derive from "an external code of divine commandments," or is it man-made, something that can be "forged through individual and group experience"?

_____

_____

_____

4. What feature makes humans different from other living creatures as well as from nonliving things? Illustrate with examples, if you can.

_____

_____

_____

5. "The presence of moral disagreement does not indicate the absence of universal morality." Do you agree with this statement? Why or why not?

_____

_____

_____

6. What evidence is there to show that morality is universal? Do you agree that "relativism in its pure sense simply does not exist"? Why or why not?

_____

_____

_____

7. What is the relationship between God and the concept of absolute morality? Explain your response.

_____

_____

_____

8. How do atheists attempt to use evolution in order to give a secular explanation for morality? How does the theory of kin selection explain altruistic and sacrificial behavior?

_____

_____

_____

9. Explain the merits of the theory of reciprocal altruism. What does this theory explain, and what does it leave unexplained?

_____

_____

_____

10. Identify the strange distinguishing features of morality that are listed in the last few paragraphs of the chapter. Do you agree with these, and can you think of other unusual aspects about the moral voice we all possess within us?

_____

_____

_____

THE GHOST IN THE MACHINE: WHY MAN IS MORE THAN MATTER

1. Because the soul cannot be located within the body in the same way that brains, arteries, blood, and organs can, where is the soul? Explain your answer.

   _____

   _____

   _____

2. Atheist Daniel Dennett doesn't entirely deny the soul, but he says it is simply a name for the brain's ability to do certain kinds of mechanical processing. Do you agree? Why or why not?

   _____

   _____

   _____

3. Physicist Jerome Elbert gives two reasons for why the notion of an immaterial soul makes him uneasy. Why, as a scientist, does Elbert feel these qualms?

_____

_____

_____

4. According to biologists Francis Crick and E. O. Wilson, if man is merely a material being subject to physical laws, it follows that free will is an illusion. Is this true? Explain your response.

_____

_____

_____

5. Richard Dawkins contends that although our genes are selfish, we ourselves don't have to be. He argues that we can rebel against the tyranny of our selfish genes. Do you think Dawkins is being consistent here? Explain.

_____

_____

_____

6. What's wrong with cognitive psychologist Steven Pinker's argument that we can declare ourselves independent of our genetic programming?

_____

_____

_____

7. My brain doesn't see or hear or believe or make interpretations.
   I do. What is the significance of this distinction?

   _____

   _____

   _____

8. How do we experience the outside world differently than
   we experience ourselves? How does philosopher Arthur
   Schopenhauer use the existence of this "inside information"
   to criticize materialism?

   _____

   _____

   _____

9. How does our human subjective experience of thinking and
   feeling and hearing music differ from the materialist understanding of such experiences?

   _____

   _____

   _____

10. What features of our humanity show the limits of a purely
    material understanding of mankind?

    _____

    _____

    _____

11. Biologist J. B. S. Haldane writes, "If my mental processes are determined wholly by the motions of atoms in my brain, I have no reason to suppose my beliefs are true . . . and hence I have no reason for supposing my brain to be composed of atoms."[19] Discuss this thought.

   _____

   _____

   _____

12. How does the presence of free will undermine the premise that we are material objects entirely comprehensible in terms of scientific laws?

   _____

   _____

   _____

13. If there is a "ghost in the machine," which we term the soul, why is it that the soul has no specific location within the body?

   _____

   _____

   _____

14. Having read this chapter, what response would you give to someone who denied that human beings have a soul?

   _____

   _____

   _____

THE IMPERIAL "I": WHEN THE SELF BECOMES THE ARBITER OF MORALITY

1. What do the terms "traditional morality" and "secular morality" bring to mind? Give some examples of each.

   _____

   _____

   _____

2. Though secular morality repudiates Christian assumptions, it nevertheless shows a kinship with Christianity. What are the similarities and differences between traditional Christianity and secular morality?

   _____

   _____

   _____

3. Show how secular morality derives from Rousseau's idea that humanity's original goodness has been corrupted by society. How did Rousseau depart from the Christian idea of original sin?

_____

_____

_____

4. How do self-disclosure and confession function within secular morality? How does this compare to the role of self-disclosure and confession in traditional Christianity?

_____

_____

_____

5. Do you know people who live by a secular moral code? If so, what are some of their distinguishing characteristics?

_____

_____

_____

6. How do divorce rates illustrate the contemporary force of secular morality?

_____

_____

_____

7. What is the assumption at the heart of the secular ethic of the inner self? Is this assumption true or false?

_____

_____

_____

8. In what respect is original sin a Christian doctrine that can be accepted whether or not one is a Christian?

_____

_____

_____

9. Do you agree that we should not completely repudiate secular morality? Why or why not? What other options are available?

_____

_____

_____

OPIATE OF THE MORALLY CORRUPT: WHY UNBELIEF IS SO APPEALING

1. Think about Karen Armstrong's statement that "it is wonderful not to have to cower before a vengeful deity, who threatens us with eternal damnation if we do not abide by his rules."[20] What does this say about a possible motivation for rejecting God?

    _____

    _____

    _____

2. Many atheists attribute their rejection of God to an absence of evidence. Why is this an incomplete or inadequate explanation of atheistic motives?

    _____

    _____

    _____

3. Atheists typically explain the motives of religious believers by appealing to the idea of wish fulfillment. Why is this an implausible explanation of Judaism and Christianity?

_____

_____

_____

4. Consider philosopher Thomas Nagel's confession: "I want atheism to be true. . . . It isn't just that I don't believe in God. . . . I don't want there to be a God; I don't want the universe to be like that."[21] What are some possible reasons for holding such a view?

_____

_____

_____

5. Why is it paradoxical to find champions of evolution so serene— and even gleeful—about living in a world where there is no higher being and man is on an uninterrupted continuum with the animals? Does this seem strange to you? Why or why not?

_____

_____

_____

6. Did Darwin lose his faith when he discovered evolution? If not, can we distinguish Darwin's scientific work from his personal rejection of God? How?

_____

_____

_____

7. How can the atheist rejection of God be traced back to ancient thinkers such as Epicurus and Lucretius? Why does this matter to Christians today?

_____

_____

_____

8. Explain how "Darwinism becomes a way to break free of the confines of traditional morality." Do you agree or disagree?

_____

_____

_____

9. What does poet Czeslaw Milosz mean when he writes that "a true opium of the people is a belief in nothingness after death"?[22]

_____

_____

_____

10. "Atheism . . . is the opiate of the morally corrupt." Does this mean that all atheists are immoral? Explain your answer.

_____

_____

_____

11. Friedrich Nietzsche sought a reversal of values in which things previously considered wrong might now be considered right. Do you think this is already happening in Western society? If so, give examples.

_____

_____

_____

12. "Man has killed God in order to win for himself the freedom to make his own morality." What does this statement imply about Nietzsche's famous phrase "God is dead"? Does it refer only to God's existence being in doubt, or does it mean more than that? Explain your answer.

_____

_____

_____

13. What does it mean to say that much of today's atheism can be understood as "a pelvic revolt against God"?

_____

_____

_____

14. How have the sexual revolution and abortion contributed to the incentive to get rid of God?

_____

_____

_____

15. In what ways are bioethicist Peter Singer's controversial views on infanticide, euthanasia, and animal rights derived from his Darwinian atheism?

    _____

    _____

    _____

16. Do you agree that "if America were a purely secular society, there would be no moral debate about child killing"? Why or why not?

    _____

    _____

    _____

17. "The atheist seeks to get rid of moral judgment by getting rid of the judge." Describe how this strategy might be appealing to young people who are for the first time experiencing the freedom of living away from their parents.

    _____

    _____

    _____

THE PROBLEM OF EVIL: WHERE IS ATHEISM WHEN BAD THINGS HAPPEN?

1. Is the "problem of evil" based on questioning God's omnipotence, his compassion, or both? Explain.

   _____

   _____

   _____

2. Why might the problem of evil and suffering not be a problem for Hinduism and Buddhism?

   _____

   _____

   _____

3. Why is the problem of evil also a problem for atheists?

_____

_____

_____

4. What do you see as the central objective of this chapter? Explain.

_____

_____

_____

5. Name a couple of tragedies from recent times. (If you prefer, recall a tragedy in your own life.) Discuss what the atheist point of view offers in helping people cope with tragedy.

_____

_____

_____

6. What do you think philosopher William James was getting at with his "pragmatic" defense of religion? What does religion offer that atheism doesn't?

_____

_____

_____

7. Why is materialism inconsistent with our experience of tragedy as horribly unjust?

_____

_____

_____

8. In answering Job's questions in the Bible, God reminds Job that
    he is merely a mortal man who didn't create the universe and
    cannot comprehend the ways of God. This satisfies Job, but
    would it satisfy you? Is it a good argument to offer someone
    who is not a Christian? Why or why not?

    _____

    _____

    _____

9. How does free will help to explain why God might allow people
    such as Hitler, Mao, and serial killers to inflict grave harm on
    others?

    _____

    _____

    _____

10. Does God's foreknowledge of the terrible things that people are
    going to do make Him complicit in those actions? Explain.

    _____

    _____

    _____

11. Free will can help account for moral evil but it cannot account
    for natural evil. Why would a just God allow earthquakes,
    tsunamis, and cancer?

    _____

    _____

    _____

12. How does the Christian concept of eternal life help to put the problem of natural evil and suffering in perspective?

_____

_____

_____

13. How do Christians respond in the face of terrible tragedy? How should we respond?

_____

_____

_____

PART VIII

CHRISTIANITY AND YOU

JESUS AMONG OTHER GODS: THE UNIQUENESS OF CHRISTIANITY

1. What two types of people say that all religions are basically the same? Why do they say this? How would you respond to each type of person?

   _____

   _____

   _____

2. Give some examples to show how the major religions differ from one another. What makes Christianity unique?

   _____

   _____

   _____

3. What is the universal problem, outlined by Pascal, that all religions seek to address?

_____

_____

_____

4. Compare and contrast the unflattering view of human nature shared by Christianity and Darwinism.

_____

_____

_____

5. What is the Hindu and Buddhist solution to the problem of the flawed self?

_____

_____

_____

6. How do Judaism and Islam seek to cross the enormous chasm between man and God?

_____

_____

_____

7. What is the Christian critique of the solutions proposed by other religions?

_____

_____

_____

8. What is the importance of the "incredible sacrifice" of God becoming man?

_____

_____

_____

9. What does C. S. Lewis mean when he writes that Christ "offers everything for nothing"? What do we have to do to win salvation through Christ? Why do you think people resist this?

_____

_____

_____

10. Atheist Christopher Hitchens says he doesn't want to go to heaven, because heaven to him sounds like "celestial North Korea." Do you want to go to heaven? What does heaven seem like to you?

_____

_____

_____

11. "The gates of hell are locked from the inside." Discuss what this statement means to you.

_____

_____

_____

12. What does it mean to say that salvation is not the gift *from* God but rather the gift *of* God? Why would we want such a gift? Explain your response.

   _____

   _____

   _____

A FORETASTE OF ETERNITY: HOW CHRISTIANITY CAN CHANGE YOUR LIFE

1. Do you know people who are full of questions about God and Christianity? Consider the example of the man who approached John Stott with questions. What does this story tell you about how to respond to the problem of unbelief? Do you think Stott should have refused to answer the man's questions? Why or why not?

    _____

    _____

    _____

2. Make a list of the five people you think have most influenced human history. Explain your choices. From a purely human point of view, without considering Jesus as God, how would you rank him on that list?

    _____

    _____

    _____

3. "The history of the West . . . is incomprehensible without Christ, and would be unimaginably different had he not lived." Try to envision how things might have been different if Christ had never walked the earth, both for you personally and for the world in general. Discuss.

_____

_____

_____

4. What is the evidence, apart from the Bible, that Christ was a historical figure, that he actually existed? Can we trust the Bible to give a reliable account of Christ's life, death, and resurrection? Support your answer.

_____

_____

_____

5. Give three pieces of evidence you would present to an atheist who said, "The Resurrection is a complete myth. I cannot believe that such nonsense ever actually happened."

_____

_____

_____

6. What is meant by the statement that "Christ is the most divisive figure who has ever lived"? Is this a good thing? Do you agree with this description? Why or why not? Have you ever personally experienced divisiveness based on your faith? If so, explain.

_____

_____

_____

7. Atheist Richard Dawkins writes that Christ did not claim any kind of divine status. What evidence can you cite from the four Gospels to show that Dawkins is wrong?

_____

_____

_____

8. Why is it important to consider the practical benefits for our lives of becoming Christians? What are these practical benefits? Which of them have you experienced, and which is most important to you? Can you think of others that belong on the list?

_____

_____

_____

9. Consider the phrase *sub specie aeternitatis*. What does it mean? Has this idea had an influence in your life? If so, give some examples.

_____

_____

_____

10. How would you respond to the atheists' claim that by focusing on the next life, Christians make this life insignificant if not irrelevant? In what way do Christians hold this life to be crucially important?

_____

_____

_____

11. How would you respond to someone who is terrified of death?

_____

_____

_____

12. How is the Christian concept of marriage different from the secular concept of marriage? If you're married, how has your marriage been affected by your faith?

_____

_____

_____

13. The book concludes with a description of earthly happiness as a foretaste of eternity and an expression of hope for the return of Jesus. Do you eagerly await that return? Are you ready? Explain.

_____

_____

_____

14. Do you believe that reading this book has prepared you to be ready with an answer to those who do not believe as you do? Explain.

_____

_____

_____

NOTES

1. Stephen Pinker, *How the Mind Works* (New York: Penguin, 1997), 555.
2. Wendy Kaminer, "Our Very Own Taliban," *American Prospect*, online edition, September 17, 2001; http://www.prospect.org/cs/articles?article=our_very_own_taliban.
3. These were Carl Sagan's opening words on *Cosmos*, the television series he hosted on PBS, beginning in 1980.
4. Sam Harris, *Letter to a Christian Nation* (New York: Knopf, 2006), 73.
5. Alexander Moszkowski, *Conversations with Einstein* (New York: Horizon, 1971), 46.
6. Richard Dawkins, *Unweaving the Rainbow* (Boston: Houghton Mifflin, 1998), 5.
7. Stephen M. Barr, *Modern Physics and Ancient Faith* (Notre Dame, IN: University of Notre Dame Press, 2003), 157.
8. Paul Davies, *The Mind of God: The Scientific Basis for a Rational World* (New York: Touchstone Books, 1993), 81.
9. Douglas Erwin, cited by Kenneth Chang, "In Explaining Life's Complexity, Darwinists and Doubters Clash," *New York Times*, August 22, 2005.
10. Richard Lewontin, "Billions and Billions of Demons," *New York Review of Books*, vol. 44, no. 1, January 9, 1997.
11. Neil deGrasse Tyson and Donald Goldsmith, *Origins* (New York: Norton, 2004), 19.

12. John 20:29.
13. Christopher Hitchens, "Mommie Dearest," Slate.com, October 20, 2003; http://www.slate.com/id/2090083.
14. Steven Weinberg, *Facing Up: Science and Its Cultural Adversaries* (Cambridge, MA: Harvard University Press, 2001), 242.
15. Henry Kamen, *The Spanish Inquisition: A Historical Revision* (New Haven, CT: Yale University Press, 1997), 305.
16. Richard Dawkins, *The God Delusion* (Boston: Houghton Mifflin, 2006), 315.
17. See, for example, http://www.stephenjaygould.org/ctrl/quotes_hitler.html.
18. Author's paraphrase.
19. J. B. S. Haldane, *Possible Worlds* (London: Chatto and Windus, 1927), 209.
20. Karen Armstrong, *A History of God* (New York: Ballantine, 1993), 378.
21. Thomas Nagel, *The Last Word* (New York: Oxford University Press, 1997), 130.
22. Czeslaw Milosz, "The Discreet Charm of Nihilism," *New York Review of Books,* vol. 45, no. 18, November 19, 1998.